THE SAINT VALENTINE'S DAY MASSACRE

THE GRIPPING TALE OF PROHIBITIONS WORST MASSACRE

JOHN FLEURY

Absolute Crime Press
ANAHEIM, CALIFORNIA

Copyright © 2019 by Minute Help, Inc.

All rights reserved. No part of this publication may be reproduced, distributed or transmitted in any form or by any means, including photocopying, recording, or other electronic or mechanical methods, without the prior written permission of the publisher, except in the case of brief quotations embodied in critical reviews and certain other noncommercial uses permitted by copyright law.

Contents

About Absolute Crime 1
Prologue 2
Prohibition and 1920s Chicago 5
Al Capone 14
The North Side Gang 23
St. Valentine's Day Massacre 32
The Discovery 44
The Investigation 48
Bibliography 65

ABOUT ABSOLUTE CRIME

Absolute Crime publishes only the best true crime literature. Our focus is on the crimes that you've probably never heard of, but you are fascinated to read more about. With each engaging and gripping story, we try to let readers relive moments in history that some people have tried to forget.

Remember, our books are not meant for the faint at heart. We don't hold back--if a crime is bloody, we let the words splatter across the page so you can experience the crime in the most horrifying way!

If you enjoy this book, please visit our homepage (www.AbsoluteCrime.com) to see other books we offer; if you have any feedback, we'd love to hear from you!

Prologue

St Valentine's Day, 1929. Chicago. North Clark Street, the Lincoln Park neighbourhood. It's the morning and the sound of a distressed dog barking cuts through it.

The sound of the dog is coming from a garage. Boarding houses sit across the street from the garage. They are run by two women. One of the women is Mrs Landesman.

Feeling agitated and slightly concerned about why the dog was making so much noise

— it had begun to howl after a short time — Mrs Landesman called to one of her roomers. He was a polite young man who immediately obeyed Mrs Landesman.

The man made his way across the street. Mrs Landesman watched him through her window. She saw him disappear into the garage and waited a moment.

The dog continued to bark. She was about to turn away with the expectation of the dog being quietened and the young roomer returning when she noticed him stumble back out into the morning. He stood on the street with his hand against the wall, steadying himself. Horror was etched across his pale face. He looked as though he'd seen a ghost.

Still the dog barked and when she saw the man throw up Mrs Landesman knew that something was seriously wrong.

[1]
PROHIBITION AND 1920S CHICAGO

January 16, 1919. The Eighteenth Amendment of the United States Constitution was announced. This was the Prohibition of alcohol, meaning a national ban on the sale, manufacture and transportation of alcohol. This would come into effect exactly one year later. America, though, wasn't ready for prohibition, nor did it want it. America was experiencing the Jazz Age and Americans were enjoying the party. Alcohol was welcomed with open arms. Prohibition was not invited.

January 17, 1920. Legitimate establishments that served alcohol are forced to close their businesses. A ripple of restlessness began to simmer among the American people. The opposite feeling simmered among the gangsters, however. Light bulb moments shone above the heads of each gang member like saintly halos. Dollar signs lit up their eyes. There was money to be made.

The prohibitionists were quick to feebly express how alcohol consumption had decreased considerably. No one was fooled. Of course it had. What choice did they have? But this obvious fact was a mere mask. Behind that mask was hidden the true fact. A fact that prohibitionists had anticipated, but could never have expected to rise as rapidly as it did. Beads of sweat trickled down the faces of the prohibitionists' faces. Beads of sweat that indicated nerves that had been jangled by the reality: Organised crime was on the rise all around the country and they didn't have the knowhow or the manpower to prevent it.

# # #

The roaring twenties. Gangsters in major cities all over the U.S. roared into action when

Prohibition came into everyone's lives. None became more famous than Chicago.

The Genna Brothers. Or the 'Terrible Gennas' as the six of them were known locally. They were a mean Sicilian crime family unit that led a ruthless gang from their base in Little Italy. Their ruthless alacrity made them the first in Chicago to capitalise on the illegal production of alcohol. Head of the family was Angelo. Handsome, piercing dark eyes and slicked back hair. It was on his orders that the Gennas jumped on the growing bandwagon.

The family made their money by extorting the wealthy. But fuelled by a hunger for more money and to be the first in Chicago to produce and sell alcohol during Prohibition, Angelo and the family decided to cut corners and get their alcohol out to the public as soon as they could. They produced industrial-grade alcohol, which wasn't palatable. In order to make it so Angelo's idea was to put additives into the mix. Reckless and conniving, the Gennas got it out to public demand. Whatever was wanted, bourbon, gin, it didn't matter. They labelled the same alcohol any way they wanted.

After all, who was going to argue with a notoriously sinister crime family? Especially when it was still alcohol they were getting. What the public and the Gennas didn't know though was that their produce would eventually leave drinkers with psychosis.

The brothers' base was Taylor Street. This was known to many as 'The Patch'. The Gennas were able to continue their sales because the police were bribed. But 'The Patch' wouldn't be the only patch in Chicago to exploit the laxity of the cops, Other gangsters soon got wind of the Genna brothers' increasing wealth. And they wanted a slice of the pie.

Big Jim Colosimo. A fearsome Italian-American Mafia boss. Stocky in stature and smart in appearance with short black hair and a thick moustache. He was a notorious gambling racketeer and whoremaster. Word got around that he had forged links with the Genna brothers.

May 11, 1920. Three weeks had passed since Big Jim had married for the second time. In the lobby of his self-named restaurant on South Wabash Avenue the crime boss waited for a shipment. The shipment never arrived. Instead, there was a delivery of spraying bullets through the entrance. Big Jim was found murdered. Nobody was ever charged, but the prime suspect was Frankie Yale. He worked for Johnny 'The Brain' Torrio.

# # #

Torrio wasn't nicknamed 'The Brain' for nothing. The avuncular-looking Papa Johnny, as he was also sometimes known, targeted Big Jim on purpose because he wanted to make a point out of him. He wanted to send out the message that he was muscling in on the flourishing alcohol business. He was willing to cooperate, but if other gangs weren't willing to comply he was willing to let things turn ugly. He had the attention of the Gennas. Torrio knew he would gain this by topping off Big Jim and instantly brokered a deal. He couldn't target Angelo or any of the other Genna brothers. If he had done that then a war would have been instigated immediately. Torrio wanted to get rich, not die trying.

Torrio's deal proposal was to divide the city's Prohibition wealth among the gangs of Chicago. He wanted the city drawn up into territories that each gang would run. This would be their "patch". Every gang, including the Gennas, agreed.

The only gang that didn't agree was the South Side O'Donnell Gang. A short time after their refusal Torrio demonstrated how powerful he was by getting the entire gang wiped off the map of Chicago. It wasn't long afterwards that the Gennas and Unione Siciliana – a Sicilian-American organisation that had strong links to the American political figures and the Mafia – partnered Torrio and his gang.

'The Brain's' tactics had worked. He was now king of Chicago.

# # #

Torrio and the Gennas were in big business. The brothers produced the alcohol and were content with the money they made from Torrio, who bought it off them. Torrio made his wealth by branching out. He brought in mass shipments of Canadian liquor. Over time Torrio's personal fortune expanded to more than $10 million per year because he was still heavily involved in the gambling and prostitution business.

The Gennas had the idea of spreading business to the Gold Coast. Profit in this part of town was booming. Torrio mulled this over. While he was doing so word got out to the North Side Gang. Dean O'Banion, a strong Irish-American mobster, vowed to fight them for their "patch" if they invaded. Torrio didn't want bloodshed so he backed away to keep the peace.

But O'Banion was pissed off. He accused Torrio and his men of breaching the agreement between the gangs. So O'Banion cheated Torrio out of $500,000 in a brewery deal and then got rid of 'The Brain' by having him arrested.

Torrio was incensed. And so he issued the order of O'Banion's murder.

November 10, 1924. The body of O'Banion was found in his North Side flower shop. His corpse was covered in bullet holes. The pretty flora had been redecorated with the colour of his blood. The North Side Gang was livid. They wanted the blood of Torrio in revenge, and to get to him they were willing to spill the blood of any man that blocked their path to him.

A gang war started that day in November.

# # #

January 24, 1925. Torrio was in the car on South Clyde Avenue with his wife, Anna. They were returning home from a shopping trip. They never made it home that day though.

Instead their car was met with a hail of gunfire from the weapons of Hymie Weiss, Vincent Drucci and Bugs Moran. The three men were members of the North Side Gang and they'd managed to track the rival gang's leader down. Defenceless, Torrio was hit in the jaw, lungs, groin, legs and abdomen. While Torrio bled heavily Moran stepped forward. Through the shattered glass of the car window he placed the barrel of his gun to the temple of 'The Brain.' He pulled the trigger but nothing happened. To his chagrin Moran had run out of ammunition. To his luck Torrio's life was spared. The sound of sirens indicated their time to escape so the three men fled.

In hospital Torrio had to undergo emergency surgery. Post-surgery he was strapped to a life support machine. His men kept a round the clock vigil. Over time he made a recovery. When he'd slowly regained his strength he kept omertà, the gangland principle of maintaining a code of silence from the authorities. Instead Torrio summoned his protégé.

To his protégé Torrio announced his retirement. The king of Chicago was bowing out and it was time for his prince to take to the throne.

Torrio's heir to the throne was Al Capone.

[2]
AL CAPONE

Al Capone, the most well-known of American gangsters. If Torrio was the king of Chicago, then Capone was to become the God. With his dark dapper three-piece suits complete with fashionable wide lapels coupled with his heavy-set frame and dark features, Capone was able to look both menacing and elegant. When he took over Torrio's gang they were known as the Chicago Outfit. But he was so successful as a gang boss they soon became known simply as the Capones. They were his family. They were his brothers. They were his life.

Before all that though Capone was based in New York. He was born to Italian immigrants Gabriele and Teresina in Brooklyn in 1899. Capone was one of nine children; he had six brothers and two sisters. Though Capone was a bright child school didn't interest him. Hustlers, crooks and money did. So it was unsurprising that he was expelled at the age of 14 for striking his female teacher in the face. He got himself a job in the local bowling alley, which is where he met Johnny Torrio.

A bond was forged between the pair immediately. Capone idolised the gangster and Torrio liked the promise shown in the kid. So he took him under his wing. When Capone reached his early twenties he learned that Torrio was moving to Chicago to infiltrate the wealth being generated by the trade in illegal alcohol. For him it was a no-brainer. Torrio was more of a father figure to him than Gabriele had ever been. And there was serious money to be made in Chicago. So Capone followed Torrio and the gang.

Capone had been involved with several small-time gangs back in New York while he was growing up. He was a part of the Junior Forty Thieves, the Bowery Boys, the Brooklyn Rippers and the Five Points Gang who had quite a reputation in Lower Manhattan. He liked the solidarity between the gang members. He enjoyed the rush he felt when they pulled off jobs. He had a taste for the money they made and the girls they attracted. He got a thrill from the sense of danger felt when in fights with other gangs. He was even secretly proud of the scar he had on the left side of his face.

This scar was gained from an attack made on him by Frank Gallucio, who defended his sister whom Capone had insulted. Capone's then employee Frankie Yale made Capone apologise to Gallucio. Later on in Chicago Capone would go on to hire Gallucio as his bodyguard. After all, it was thanks to him that Capone had gained the menacing appearance and sobriquet which he was especially proud of: Scarface.

# # #

So Capone followed Torrio and his men to Chicago, leaving behind his young wife Mae and their infant son, Albert Francis, otherwise nicknamed Sonny. They would move to be with him at a later date. In the new city and his new home Capone showed how gutsy and reliable he was, and Torrio was proved right in believing in his potential.

One of the first things that needed to be taken care of when they arrived was assisting Torrio's cousin's husband with the problem he was having with the Black Hand. The Black Hand was a notorious extortion racket that had roots dating back to the Kingdom of Naples of the 1750s. With no intention of negotiating Torrio and Capone approached this the same way as they had done with Colosimo: Execute them. And that they did. No words, just cold-blooded murder. This, coupled with the execution of Big Jim, stamped their mark on to the heart of Chicago. It was their way of announcing their arrival. They were there simply to rake in the green of the dollar and were willing to paint the town red with blood if necessary.

This willingness to fight and commitment to sacrifice if required shown by Capone impressed Torrio. He was further impressed in 1924.

The young Capone got himself involved in the council elections that were held in Cicero. It didn't take long for word to spread about the corruption of these elections and that Capone was the mastermind behind them all. They later became known as one of the most rigged elections in the history of the United States. Voters within the township were threatened by Capone and his thugs at the polling stations. Unsurprisingly, the mayoral candidate whom Capone was backing won by an enormous margin.

Weeks later the mayor and Capone fell out so the mayor went public in an effort to get the complete backing of the people. He vowed to run Capone out of town. Shortly after this announcement they came face-to-face on the steps of the town hall. In front of crowds of people Capone knocked the mayor down the steps. This demonstrated his fearlessness. This demonstration made him a reason to be feared. Looking down upon his puppet-mayor while he was lying at the bottom of the steps was a hugely symbolic act. It marked Capone as the one who was truly pulling the strings.

This didn't go unnoticed by Torrio who merely smiled at the development of his protégé.

# # #

Torrio may have been nicknamed 'The Brain' but Capone clearly demonstrated that he had one too. It was under his control that a successful transport network was established for the smuggled liquor. He established trusted links with the rum-runners of the East Coast, the Purple Gang in Detroit and Midwestern moonshine producers. And these were just a pinch out of the large bag of sugar that was the Prohibition-era illegal liquor trade. Capone was largely responsible for making the gang grow rich. It was estimated that they raked in around $100 million per year in revenue. Through his wealth Capone was able to move his family over and set up headquarters in the Lexington Hotel. This became known as 'Capone's Castle.'

After the attack on Torrio and the handover to Capone, 'Scarface' decided to stamp his authority all over the city. He wanted it as his own. He wanted more. He strengthened his stronghold over the politicians by bribing the city's mayor, William 'Big Bill' Hale Thompson. He paid off the police so that he could operate without their intrusion. He expanded into the casino business. He operated speakeasies.

With his money he bought himself flashy jewellery, big time pieces and the most expensive cigars. He wore luxurious custom-made suits. He dined out every night in the finest restaurants. He was charitable and regularly donated money to the poor. He opened soup kitchens for the homeless and unemployed. He attracted the attention of everyone, including the media. And he lapped up the limelight. Within no time of becoming the gang's new boss Al Capone became a celebrity figure.

This was what was seen at face value though. Deeper than that Capone was ruthless, and he applied these methods to anyone unwilling to let him get his way. Like a bully, this was how Capone got his wealth, status and omnipotent power. But with his mind focused on growing the business and his fortune it seemed as though he'd forgotten the North Side Gang who had forced his mentor into retirement. Or had he?

Capone knew exactly what he was doing. He may have been a thug, but he was definitely smart. Each time he gained something new or appeared in the media he knew the North Side Gang would be watching, just like everybody else. And he knew this would infuriate them, which it did. The North Side Gang was expecting Capone to hit back at them immediately. But he didn't. And this angered them to their core because while they were waiting for him he was busy eating up every business in Chicago.

September 20, 1926. Capone and his entourage were lunching in the Hawthorne Hotel restaurant. Everyone was in good spirits. Everyone was enjoying themselves in the busy and pleasant atmosphere. All of a sudden though, the ambience was shattered. Literally. Glass and wood imploded amidst an explosion of bullets fired from the Thompson submachine guns and shotguns lined up on the street outside. Several people were injured, including everyday civilians. There was no denying who was responsible for the shootings. There was no denying who the intended target was.

Capone paid for the medical care for those injured. He then approached the North Side Gang with hope of reaching some kind of reconciliation. Shaken, infuriated, and seeking peace, Capone offered a truce. The men weren't interested though. They wanted to fight. They hated Capone and weren't afraid of him. They never had been. They wanted him out of the city. They wanted him dead. Forget the truce, this was war. And with that Capone was forced to walk away.

Shaken, infuriated, and now humiliated. Capone began to plot his next move.

[3]
THE NORTH SIDE GANG

Otherwise known as the North Side Mob, the North Side Gang were the Chicago Outfit's biggest rivals during Prohibition. They were Irish-Americans. A band of brothers. What gang wasn't? But they allowed Polish-Americans into their gang. They were willing to extend the family unlike most other gangs.

The members grew up on the streets of Chicago. They knew their city like no-one else. Most of them grew up together in a mob called the Market Street Gang. Petty thieves. Pick pockets. Labour sluggers. These were the titles that belonged to the boys of the Market Street Gang. When they grew up it was like moving on into high school. The boys became the men of the North Side Gang.

Their leader was Dean O'Banion. He specialised in bootlegging and racketeering. He was also a florist. This legitimate business was a mask that hid his other money-making schemes. Schemes that weren't so legitimate. Like Capone, O'Banion also had a mentor. Charles 'The Ox' Reiser. He was a safecracker who was also a mentor to other boys like Bugs Moran and Hymie Weiss. Under his guidance the boys became men. Hardened gangsters who took no shit. This was what made them so fearless of Torrio and Capone.

When Prohibition came the gang already had a reputation for themselves. There were no worthy opponents in the north side of Chicago. It was easy for them to take control of the existing breweries and distilleries.

They operated from McGovern's Saloon and Café on North Clark Street. The neighbourhoods in the 42nd and 43rd Wards were their 'patches'. Not only did the gang make money from bootlegging, they also got rich from running illegal gambling dens and burglarising local businesses. It seemed old habits die hard.

O'Banion drew a lot of similarities to Capone. He too had a stronghold on local politicians. But O'Banion hated Italians. And he liked his voice and insults to be heard. It was this hatred and his greed that led to his murder by the Chicago Outfit in his beloved floristry.

# # #

With O'Banion dead it was left to Weiss, Moran and Drucci to lead the North Side Gang. Torrio was out of the game, the three had made sure of that. Capone was shaken. The three laughed when they learned 'Scarface' had ordered an armoured vehicle be made especially for him after they rejected his call for a truce. They knew they had gained the upper hand. They could taste the fear and they wanted more.

While Capone kept his head down the deadly triumvirate went after everyone around him. First on their hit list was Angelo Genna. Moran tracked him down. In his vehicle, on the road, he wasted no time. He pulled out his gun. Genna spotted him though, and put his foot down. A dangerous car chase through the streets of Chicago ensued. Hollywood would have been proud. Eventually Moran caught up with Genna. This time there was no escaping. Genna was blown away with several shots.

News spread. Shockwaves were felt. There were ripples of concern in the city. The Gennas were incensed. They'd lost their leader. Having lost such a close ally Capone was left even more shaken.

The North Side Gang weren't done there though. They were just getting warmed up. The Gennas had barely had time to mourn and plot before they lost another brother. This time it was Mike AKA 'The Devil'. He certainly lived up to his nickname and brought hell with him when he got himself into a shootout with the North Side Gang. The police showed up and 'The Devil' was taken down by them. He'd managed to hold off the firepower of the North Siders, but the added firepower of the law was too much for him.

The Gennas were so shocked they could only watch helplessly as their family were torn apart by these bloodthirsty Irish-Americans. Next to be gunned down was Samuzzo 'Samoots' Amatuna. He was a loyal family friend who had remained strong for them right after Angelo's murder. He'd been there for them. Kept them together. Worked hard at consoling them and keeping them strong. But his loyalty was to prove his undoing. Drucci was the man responsible for putting the bullets into Samoots's body.

The final execution was another Genna brother. This time Tony was the target. Being as Moran and Drucci had already carried out hits the honour this time was bestowed upon Weiss. He duly delivered. It was after this murder that the Gennas finally took action. It took the death of three brothers and a lifelong friend for them to respond. And they responded by fleeing Chicago.

The North Side Gang had succeeded in taking a huge scalp. The Genna family were the first in Chicago to capitalise on the Prohibition's business opportunity. With them gone the North Siders grew richer and more powerful over night by eating up the businesses they'd left behind.

They celebrated the departure of the Genna brothers. But they still weren't done. The main man was still in their city. Next on their list of targets was Al Capone.

# # #

Capone and his bodyguard were lunching together. They were in the Lexington Hotel. Capone's hotel. Finishing up their meal they headed down to the bar for a drink. It was a fine day. The men were enjoying one another's company. Little did they know their day was about to be heavily disrupted. Little did they know that a fleet of cars had pulled up outside. Little did they know the cars were filled with members of the North Side Gang, and that the gang was heavily armed with Thompson submachine guns.

The only time Capone and his bodyguard became aware was when their day was interrupted by the heavy fire. The explosive sounds came at the same time as the bullets tore through the building and raced towards them. The men threw themselves to the ground and were blanketed by broken debris and dust.

When it ended and the North Siders had left Capone swore revenge. This had been the second time an attempt had been made on his life. He had attempted to keep the peace. But now, he wanted nothing more than the death of these men.

Capone wasted no time and called upon his men. They were going after Hymie Weiss. Though he, Drucci and Moran were joint leaders, Capone felt Weiss was the brains of the three. Days after the Lexington was torn to pieces so too was Weiss. His body was found on the Chicago streets loaded with bullets. His corpse wasn't alone. Capone's men had taken down every man that was found with Weiss. When news reached Drucci and Moran it was their turn to feel a sting of pain at having lost a brother. It was their turn to call for a truce.

A meeting was held in which the two North Siders and Capone attended with several gang members. After a lengthy discussion during the conference peace was agreed. Gunfire ceased. Killings stopped. But the temptations to antagonise did not.

Alcohol shipments were hijacked. Dog tracks were burned down. These temptations were an attempt at luring the other gang into breaking the ceasefire and making them out to look the bad guy. Nobody broke though. The Cold War, as it became known, lasted for a couple of years.

After some time news reached Capone that Drucci was dead. Rubbing his hands together with glee Capone learned how his rival had been gunned down by police during a shootout with them. Two down. One to go.

Moran was the lone rival and Capone expected him to buckle under paranoia and fear. But Moran wasn't paranoid or afraid. He was hell-bent on destroying Capone. He was mad for power. He was a natural born jingoist and his next temptation at ending the ceasefire pushed Capone over the limit.

Moran ordered for the execution of two of Capone's union leaders. More than that, however, the two men were personal friends of

Capone. Moran had crossed the line, as far as Capone was concerned. He had to go.

As Capone devised his plan a thought struck him: why stop at just Moran? The entire North Side Gang had to go. Excitement grew as the possibility of the plan working unfolded before his eyes. His plan was no execution. It was a massacre.

With all the details configured all that was left was to choose the day. And that day was going to be St. Valentine's Day.

[4]
St. Valentine's Day Massacre

February 14, 1929. St. Valentine's Day. It was a fresh clear morning. The neighbourhood was alive. People had begun their days. Young lovers walked down the sidewalk holding hands. Others stuck at work dreamed idly of their partners.

2122 North Clark Street. Located in the Lincoln Park neighbourhood. Chicago's North Side. It was 10:30 am. The SMC Cartage warehouse, which doubled up as a garage, was the destination for members of the North Side Gang. They had been in contact with Detroit's Purple Gang. The Detroit mob had promised a cut-price deal on a huge shipment of stolen whiskey. This was the big bucks. Moran and his men wanted in. They thought their luck was in and they were going to laugh all the way to the bank. With this deal pulled off Moran wished he could be a fly on the wall in Capone's office just to see the look on his face. The North Siders laughed about this. Things were going right. They'd lost two leading soldiers in Weiss and Drucci, but the gang was still intact. Soon they'd get Capone and his goons out of the way. And they'd become the kings of Chicago. Rightful heirs to their beloved city. The city they had called home since they could talk. As far as they were concerned Al Capone and his mob were nothing but intruders.

The day started early for the North Side Gang. They got to the warehouse early to meet the huge shipment. They had all woken up with the same feeling. A feeling of pending wealth that excited them. A feeling that was coupled with a thrill they would surely feel at having pulled off the heist. A feeling of gratitude towards the Purple Gang for wanting to strike the deal with them instead of Capone.

The gang all wanted to be part of the day. They all wanted to share the experience and do their part for the good of the gang. They were going to chip in and get their hands on their rightful share.

The gang called in the help of two associates: Peter and Frank Gusenberg. The brothers were loyal enforcers to the gang. They had carried out their duties presented to them by Moran so efficiently and so diligently that Moran considered them part of the family. They were reliable. They could be trusted. And whenever the gang needed an extra set of hands they were the first Moran would turn to.

The German-American brothers were expert contract killers, too. They worked together in performing the perfect executions. They were feared throughout the city, not just because of their reputation, but because of their imposing bulk, unflinching gaze and menacing snarls. Their expertise was called upon when the executions were carried out on the Genna brothers and they were part of the gang when the assassination attempts had been carried out on Capone.

As efficient as always, the pair were at the warehouse on Valentine's Day morning at the exact time specified. Their punctuality always ensured they arrived on the dot. The Gusenberg brothers' arrival was met by North Side Gang members Albert Kachellek, Adam Heyer, Rinhardt Schwimmer, Albert Weinsschenker and John May.

Each member had his own particular role to play in the gang. Kachellek, sometimes known as James Clark, had been promoted to Moran's right-hand man after the death of Drucci. 'Clark' was all muscle, so he enjoyed being the boss's bodyguard. Moran felt comfortable around 'Clark,' being as he was also his brother-in-law.

Heyer went by several aliases. Although he was mostly known as Adam he was also known as Frank Meyer, Frank Snyder and John Snyder. He was an educated man and excellent with figures. It was little surprise then that he was the gang's accountant. Business and financial affairs were all left in his capable hands.

Schwimmer was an optometrist. Or so he claimed. Schwimmer was actually a failed optician with no medical training whatsoever. He'd failed at the first hurdle because his vice was gambling on horse races.

Weinschenker had an uncanny resemblance to Moran. Everybody noticed it and always commented on it. Even Moran couldn't help but notice the uncanny resemblances. Weinschenker enhanced the appearance and attracted further comments by dressing like the boss. This only led to the gang taking the mickey out of him. Secretly though, he didn't care. He liked the attention. He lapped it up, because he knew it curried favours with the boss. It never went unnoticed on Moran. Though Moran liked his little doppelganger he only made him responsible for the gang's cleaning and dyeing operations. This was the boss's way of poking his own fun at Weinschenker.

May was a misanthropic drifter. The black sheep of the gang. He kept to himself and didn't like to mingle. Although the North Side Gang looked to him as a member he sometimes disappeared for months on end. He'd come crawling back when he needed money though. Perhaps the fact that he had a wife and seven children had something to do with his miserable state. Sometimes he was hired as added muscle for certain jobs. But May had morals. He would happily fight any man. He could take care of himself. But he never carried a gun. His main role in the gang was the mechanic. He preferred the company of vehicles and engines than other people.

When all the men arrived at the warehouse they were in good spirits. All except May who remained in the background with his dog, a German shepherd named Highball. The rest of the men talked. They joked. They laughed. They waited. They were waiting for the boss who was running late.

Moran was running late because he had overslept. He was so calm in comparison to the rest of the gang that he had managed to oversleep. The others had been awake with excitement for hours. Moran casually got himself ready. When he was dressed one of the North Siders, Ted Newberry, was waiting for him in a car outside.

Together, they made their way to the warehouse.

# # #

A police car pulled up outside the rear entrance of the warehouse. At the same time, on the other side of the building, a Cadillac Sedan pulled up outside the main entrance. Four men were inside the Cadillac. All of the men emerged from the vehicle. Two of them were uniformed police officers. The policemen were armed. Shotguns were fiercely gripped in their hands. The men entered the warehouse and came face-to-face with Moran and his men.

The gang was in good spirits – laughing and chatting amongst themselves. Only John May was not a part of the jests. He had begun amending the engine of one of the trucks inside the garage space. Suddenly the voices stopped. The next set of jokes came to an abrupt halt before the punch lines could be delivered. The laughter filtered. And even May put down his tools. The gang realised they were not alone.

Without explanation as to why they were there the police officers ordered all of the men to line up against the wall. The gang did not object. Their day had begun so promisingly. They were supposed to be rich when they went to bed that night. But the police. The Goddamn police had caught wind of the transaction. And now the game was up. They'd been rumbled. As they lined up against the wall the officers noticed Moran shift a despairing look at his men around him. Unceremoniously the North Side Gang was bowing out. Dejected and hopeless Moran looked back into the eyes of the law. Nothing could be done and he knew it. This wasn't supposed to happen, his gaze told them. This is our city.

The policemen motioned to the two other men that were there with them. Plain clothed policemen no doubt, thought the North Siders. This was it. They were going to have handcuffs slapped onto their wrists. They were going to be taken in to custody and be put away for a very long time.

The plain clothed police officers did not produce handcuffs from their overcoats though. Instead, they pulled out Thompson sub-machine guns. One each. One contained a twenty-round box magazine. The other contained a fifty-round box of ammo.

The Thompson sub-machine guns were pointed at the gang lined up against the wall and for a very brief moment each man shared the same tacit expression that evolved over a few short seconds. From the initial confusion they then expressed realisation. Then the realisation transformed itself into fear.

The gunmen also shared the same expressions: Monstrous grins highlighted their evil cores.

Then the triggers on their weapons were squeezed tight and explosive sounds erupted between the police and the gangsters. The rapid sound of gunfire bounced from each wall, piercing their ears violently. The bullets fired did no bouncing, however. They merely pierced the flesh of the North Side gang members even more violently.

As the victims dropped to the ground the last image they ever saw was the demonic faces of the police lit up by the gunfire. The last sound they ever heard was the firing of the weapons that ended their existence. The last smell they ever experienced was that of the distinctive smoke produced from the guns. The last sense of feeling they ever had was that of their bodies being ripped apart viciously by the bullets, the blood spurting from the entry wounds that decorated them and the hard ground of the warehouse that caught them when they fell.

# # #

The ammo was spent. The North Side Gang was dead. Their killers looked at their corpses lying in a pool of crimson that increased in size with each second. The pool of blood was swimming towards the police. The officers in uniform stepped forward as though unafraid. They pulled up their shotguns. They wanted to play their part just as much as every North Sider wanted a part in the deal that was supposed to make them so wealthy. One shot was fired angrily from each shotgun. The blasts impacted on the heads of John May and Albert 'Clark'

Kachellek. Their faces were completely obliterated as a result. The disappearance of their identity made definitive.

After that, the four killers made their exit from the scene. A frightened-looking yet curious crowd had gathered outside. The plain clothed men came out of the building to the rear with their arms up. The uniformed police officers were close behind with their shotguns pointed at the backs of their men. Nothing to see here, they told the crowd. There had been a gun fight, they confirmed. But the men they were after had surrendered. The plain clothed men were thrown into the waiting police car and the police told the crowd to move on. Everything was resolved. Everyone should go back to what they were supposed to be doing. Relieved, the crowd moved along and the police drove away with the culprits they had arrested.

# # #

Not too far from the warehouse Capone and his men watched the scene unfold. Capone's master plan had succeeded. He was congratulated by his men while he smiled ruefully to himself. Moran and the North Side Gang had been wiped off the face of the earth. Chicago belonged to him.

# # #

Except Moran was not dead. Moran was sat comfortably in a coffee shop not far from the scene of the crime with Newberry. As Moran and Newberry approached the warehouse they had spotted the police car parked outside the building, so they had turned around and retraced their steps, finally ending up safely in a coffee shop. They waited anxiously over their coffees for news to filter through to them about what had happened.

The killer policemen were not policemen at all. They were hired killers, hired by Al Capone. And though they and Capone thought they had succeeded in their mission they had made one grave error. They had mistaken Weinschenker for Moran.

[5]
THE DISCOVERY

A dog across the road was incessantly barking. It had been for a while. Maybe the owner had left it tied up and had gone out momentarily? Whatever the reason it was distracting. And annoying. So Mrs Landesman called out to one of her young roomers who happened to be in. He was a nice young man. He'd check on the dog if she asked him. As she guessed, he agreed without any hesitation.

Such a nice young man, Mrs Landesman thought to herself while her roomer practically skipped across the street. She watched him through her window. What is wrong with that dog? she wondered.

She saw the man knock at the door. He waited for the reply. Only the desperate barks of the dog came in response. After a moment she saw him try the door and saw it open by his hand. She watched the young man step through the open door.

Inside, the building was dark. The young man called out. No-one replied. He could only hear the dog barking from the other side. The young felt his hand along the wall beside him. He found a switch and flicked it. Sleepy light lethargically came to life after an initial couple of flickers. He stepped cautiously ahead. His heart had begun racing. He had a strange feeling that something wasn't right. He called out once again. The dog barked rapidly. Pleading to him, so it seemed. Behind some dark vehicles that he bypassed there was the dog.

The young man's eyes took a couple of seconds to register what they saw. The dog was a German shepherd. Its eyes displayed sheer terror. And its coat seemed to be matted with blood.

His heart was pounding at the horror unfolding before him. He edged closer just a little more and his heart suddenly froze. There were bodies of suited men shredded apart by bullets. The blood had oozed out of their bodies to make a thick puddle along the garage floor. The dog, tied up to the corner, was trembling and shifting uneasily in the pool of blood. When the young man spotted two of the men with their faces ripped off with just a fleshy pulp left in their place he retched. One hand slapped his mouth, the other gripped his stomach. He turned and fled.

Mrs Landesman saw the man stumble back out onto the street. He was pale as a ghost. She saw him retch. He almost fell back but his hand steadied him against the wall. Something was very, very wrong. The dog continued barking in the building. What had happened? she wondered, feeling panicked. As soon as she saw the man throw up on to the sidewalk her hand was on the telephone.

She was going to call the police.

# # #

The police were at the scene not long afterwards. Every single one of them was shocked by the horror. Some of them couldn't stomach the violence and had to wait outside. To the amazement of the officers though, Highball wasn't the only survivor.

Despite fourteen bullet wounds, Frank Gusenberg was alive. Barely. The police leaned in closer. They had one question to ask him before he lost consciousness forever. Who did this?

Gusenberg's response was strained. Barely audible. Clearly it pained him to talk. But it was clear to the police what his reply was:

No-one.

Omertà.

Three hours later, Gusenberg was dead. He never revealed who was behind the atrocious murders. He, like his colleagues and brother, lived by the code. And they died by the code.

[6]
The Investigation

Police were aware of Bugs Moran's ongoing feud with Capone. They were also aware of Moran being responsible for hijacking Capone's liquor shipments from Detroit. Deciding on whether to go for Capone or the Detroit-based Purple Gang with whom Capone was so strongly tied to, police decided to target the latter. If they got their men and managed to grind them down, Capone would be brought down later.

The Chicago police managed to print off some mug shots of the known members of the Purple Gang. With the shots in hand the officers' first port of call was to visit the landlady, Mrs Landesman. Along with fellow landladies,

Mrs Orvidson and Mrs Doody, and three of their tenants – including the shaken young man who had discovered the bodies – the police officers produced the mug shots and handed them out to each individual.

As the six silently peered into the faces of the members of the Purple Gang, the police tacitly observed their reactions. It was a long shot, the police knew that. If they couldn't identify any of the men then the officers would simply thank them for their time and continue along the street. They had the day. They had intentions of stopping by every business and home along the street if necessary.

With each passing second it seemed ever more likely that this would be the case for the day. But, to the amazement of the officers, Mrs Doody and Mrs Orvidson exchanged glances with one another. They had a mutual understanding. They looked at the officers. There were four mug shots in their hands that they had agreed upon.

The mug shots were handed back to the officers. Knowing the members by name the officers looked at the shots of the men that the two women had singled out. Then it was their turn to exchange knowing looks with one another. They had to call in Jim Carrey, the van Wart brothers and 'Fletch' for questioning.

#

Carrey, Ryan and Harry van Wart, and 'Fletch' were all tracked down. Each was brought in, much to their annoyance, for questioning. From the minute they were arrested the four vehemently denied any wrongdoing. They were incensed that they had been cornered for the massacre, which by now had become national news.

Under intense scrutiny from the Chicago officers the men gave nothing away. Each was interviewed separately, yet none buckled under pressure. They all pretty much adopted the same pose – leaning back casually in their seats, some to the point of slouching. A couple crossed their arms in frustration. 'Fletch' was even so disgusted that they had wrongly been brought in that he refused to make eye contact with the law.

With each question and on the back of each interview the police came away knowing they were losing this round in the war against gangland crime. The same questions were fired at each Purple Gang member: where were they on the morning of St. Valentine's Day? What did they know of the Clark Street garage? Why had they been singled out by eye witnesses? The four men spat their matching answers back at the police. They were in Detroit that day, all they'd heard about the massacre was what news had filtered through to everyone else, and the eye witnesses were mistaken.

When police questioned them as to what news had gotten through their replies were identical: the police did it.

The Chicago officers were puzzled. The men were either telling the truth or they were professional liars. In the end, the police were left with no choice but to grudgingly release them without charge. The men walked away from the police station with smug grins plastered on their faces. The officers watched them walk away. They felt slightly disturbed. Could the Purple Gang men have been telling the truth?

Were the police really responsible for the massacre?

#

February 22, 1929. Eight days after the notorious massacre. The police were called to an incident. There had been a fire that had taken place at a garage on Wood Street. Not long after receiving the call the police arrived on the scene. When the officers discovered what had been set ablaze they suddenly realised they had a breakthrough. Their genuine first lead. A vehicle had been set alight and that vehicle was a 1927 Cadillac Sedan. This was the vehicle that had been used by the killers on St. Valentine's Day.

With increasing excitement the police were able to discover the engine number was still intact. They used these digits to trace the origins of the car. When they had done so, the Cadillac was traced back to a dealer in Michigan. The officers on the case had a trip to make.

They found the dealer and upon a short interview he told them he had sold the car to a man named James Morton. Morton was from Los Angeles, California. The police investigation also led them to discover that the Cadillac had been kept in a garage that had been rented by a man who went by the name Frank Rogers. His home address was 1859 West North Avenue. When the police tracked this address down it turned out not to be a home as initially thought, but rather a café. The Circus Café for that matter, which happened to be owned by Claude Maddox. Maddox was a former St. Louis gangster. His St. Louis gang was the well-known Egan's Rats. The Rats were known to have solid connections with Capone's organisation and the Purple Gang. Finally, it seemed, pieces of the puzzle were beginning to fit together.

As the investigation continued the police learned that there was no information on anyone who went by the names James Morton or Frank Rogers. However, a slice of luck was to come their way. That slice of luck came in the form of a truck driver named Elmer Lewis. Lewis revealed to police that early on the morning of St. Valentine's Day he had turned a corner a block away from 2122 North Clark. When he had done so his truck had sideswiped a police car. He immediately pulled over, but the uniformed driver had waved him on. This struck Lewis as peculiar, but on the policeman's orders he carried on with his journey. What stood out furthermore for the truck driver was the police driver's distinctively unprofessional appearance. Lewis mentally noted that the cop was missing a front tooth.

Police checked their files. As it so happened, somebody else had reported the accident. It had been reported by H. Wallace Caldwell, the president of the Board of Education. More than that though, Caldwell had described the uniformed policeman that had been driving the patrol car that morning. His description matched Lewis's: the cop was missing a front tooth.

The police were aware of one of Egan's Rats by the name of Fred 'Killer' Burke. Though he was part of the gang he worked particularly closely with his known partner in crime, James

Ray. Together, the pair was wanted for a robbery spree which they had carried out whilst wearing police uniforms. Burke in particular was a wanted man because of his supposed involvement in a murder that was committed during a robbery in Ohio.

Finally, the police had a strong lead. With the discovery of the burnt out Cadillac Sedan connecting them to Claude Maddox who in turn put them on the trail of the Egan's Rats gang, they had been led to 'Killer' Burke. The man had been identified by two witnesses. He'd killed before. He'd seemingly killed again. What was stopping him from committing further murders? After all, that was how he gained his nickname.

The police put everyone on the force on red alert. James 'Killer' Burke was a highly wanted man. At this stage, he was the main suspect for the St. Valentine's Day massacre.

# # #

Months passed with no further leads. Police couldn't trace Burke. He'd become the invisible man. He seemed one step ahead of them all the time. The cops knew it had something to do with Capone, but they couldn't go directly for him. His defence would be water tight. He'd have alibis, witnesses. He had politicians eating out of the palm of his hand. Hell, he even had members of the police force under his payroll. The officers on the case couldn't trust anyone, not even their closest colleagues. Everything and everyone was corrupted. Prohibition and Al Capone had tainted the city of Chicago. The investigating officers found the same questions resurfacing time and time again: what if the police force was behind the massacre?

As each month passed the case began to stagnate more and more. It was slipping through their fingers and there was no safety net. But Lady Luck was still to play her hand again. She had just been biding her time.

The night of December 14, 1929. It was a cold evening in St. Joseph, Michigan. Patrolman Charles Skelly was circling the neighbourhood. It was quiet, but it was routine procedure. People were tucked into the comfort of their warm homes preparing for Christmas. Suddenly, from behind him Skelly heard a screech of tires disrupting the night. In his rearview mirror he caught sight of a man driving erratically on the road. Losing control of his vehicle the man at the wheel rear-ended a car that was parked at the curb. Suspecting he had a drunk driver on his hands Skelly flashed the lights of his patrol car and sounded the siren.

Upon noticing there was a cop in close proximity, the man at the wheel, rather than switching off his vehicle as he should have, did just the opposite and slammed his foot down on the accelerator. He sped past patrolman Skelly and with a shake of his head the Michigan policeman had no choice but to pursue the getaway driver.

Reckless driving couldn't outrun the astute Skelly, who eventually forced the driver off the road. With the car at a standstill Skelly stepped out of his vehicle and approached the car in front. His night had not been so quiet after all. He noticed the window on the driver's side roll down. He expected to hear a spiel of protestations over the pending arrest. Instead, the driver leaned out. In his hand was a gun. Skelly froze to the spot just as three shots were fired into his body. Skelly collapsed to the ground. The driver jumped out of his wrecked car and escaped into the night on foot.

# # #

Police arrived at the scene not long after the shooting. Neighbours had been disturbed in the night by the sound of a car chase, a police siren and then shots fired. Several calls were made by frightened witnesses. By the time police got there Officer Skelly had died from his injuries. They were dealing with a murderer.

They traced the abandoned vehicle to a Frederick Dane. He was the registered owner of the car. The police recognised the name. Suspicions aroused, they made their way back to police headquarters to find out what they could about this Dane character. The officers leafed through their files at the Berrien County, Michigan Sherriff's Department. Eventually, they came to what they were searching for: Frederick Dane's files. And what they discovered was both unexpected and astonishing. Frederick Dane was an alias used by Fred 'Killer' Burke. Police photos confirmed this. Burke had certainly lived up to his nickname. And the Michigan police swore to bring the killer to justice for their fallen colleague. Skelly had not died in vain. He had led them to one of the most wanted men in America.

The Michigan police force contacted the law in Chicago with important news. Massive news in fact. Suddenly the stagnating case of the St. Valentine's Day Massacre was revived. There was hope, it seemed. Lady Luck had dealt them an important hand. Both she, and Skelly, had given them the opportunity to raid the bungalow that was registered in the name of Frederick Dane. The bungalow was based in St. Joseph, Michigan.

The Michigan police wasted no time whatsoever. A raid was organised immediately. Heavily armed the police swarmed in. Anxious neighbours peeked through the windows from behind their curtains. Ideally they wanted Burke alive. But, if he wanted to go down fighting, well, that was his choice. He was never going to win. They'd take him down before he ever got a chance to kill anyone again. The killer was now a cop killer. Every policeman at his bungalow would have loved to be the one to put a bullet in his head. End the existence of this terrible human being.

The front door of the bungalow was smashed in and amid an eruption of shouts the police raiders swarmed in. Every room was filled with armed police. They yelled out Burke's name. They called for him to surrender. They ordered him to put his hands in the air.

Except, Burke was not in the bungalow. The police, much to their vexation, had once again missed their man. Why was he always one step ahead? Nevertheless, they weren't going away empty handed. They searched every nook, crevice and cranny of his home. By the end they had amassed an enormous haul. Inside a large trunk that had been hidden away they discovered a bullet-proof vest and nearly $320,000 in bonds that had been stolen from a bank in Wisconsin. Along with this they also found a dangerous arsenal of weapons that included two Thompson submachine guns, a collection of pistols, two shotguns, and thousands of rounds of ammunition.

Back at their base the police notified the force in Chicago of what they had come away with from the raid. They may not have caught their man, but the pair of Thompson submachine guns was of huge interest to the Chicago police. They were sent for right away so they could be tested.

The era had experienced a new breakthrough in science. Forensic ballistics had given the police a major boost in tracking criminals. The guns were sent to forensics and when the news came back it was just the news they had suspected. The submachine guns were those that had been used in the St. Valentine's Day massacre. One of the 'Tommy' guns was also determined to have been used in the murder of a mobster from New York who went by the name of Frankie Yale eighteen months earlier. If Burke had been a wanted man before then that had been an understatement.

#

Missouri. More than twelve months had passed since Officer Skelly was coldly gunned down while on duty on a sleepy night in St. Joseph Michigan. It was a breezy day. Puffy white clouds passed lazily across the clear blue sky. The sun appeared white in its blistering brightness. It poured its rays down upon Bailey farm and the man that was nonchalantly digging a hole out back.

Sweating in the heat and from the physical excursion the man stopped. He wiped his brow. Then he wiped the back of his neck. Then he heard cars pull up outside the front. He wasn't expecting anybody. Filled with curiosity he casually moved towards the vehicles. Before he got a chance to reach them though a swarm of armed police stormed ahead and surrounded him.

The man was called Bailey. It was his farm.

Bailey raised his arms in the air in surrender. Where is he? demanded the police. Bailey had no choice but to give him up. He was inside. Some of the police stormed into the building while other remained outside, their eyes and guns fixed on the man.

Moments later, the police returned with the one they had come for. The unsuspecting and surprised face of Fred 'Killer' Burke met them all. Handcuffed, he was bundled into one of the police cars. The chase was over. They had finally caught one of America's most wanted criminals.

# # #

Back in Michigan Burke was sentenced to life in prison for the murder of Officer Skelly. There was not enough evidence to charge him for the St. Valentine's Day Massacre and he wouldn't confess nor testify against anyone. Omertà. Still, with him behind bars forever it was a victory for the police.

As time wore on the massacre faded more and more into the distance. No one was ever charged with the murders committed that atrocious day, which tarnished the police's small victory in the capture of Burke, who went on to die in prison in 1940.

No link was ever made back to Al Capone, who everyone knew but could not prove was behind the organisation of the St. Valentine's Day Massacre. The God of Chicago forever remained untouchable.

BIBLIOGRAPHY

Curtis, Wayne. Bootleg Paradise. April/May 2007. Report.

Blocker Jr., Jack S., Mahey, David, Tyrell, Ian R. Alcohol and Temperance in Modern History: An Global Encyclopaedia. ABC-CLIO Ltd. 2003. P. 23. Book.

Vick, Dwight. Drugs and Alcohol in the 21st Century: Theory, Behavior, and Policy. Jones and Bartlett. 2010. P. 128-129. Book.

Hendley, Nate. Al Capone: Chicago's King of Crime. Five Rivers Chapmanry. 2010. Book.

The Biography Channel. Al Capone
http://www.biography.com/people/al-capone-9237536

Bardsley, Marilyn. Al Capone: Chicago's Most Infamous Mob Boss. 2008. Report.

Keefe, Rose. Guns and Roses: The Untold Story of Dean O'Banion, Chicago's Big Shot Before Al Capone. Cumberland House. 2003. Book.

Keefe, Rose. The Man Who Got Away: The Bugs Moran Story. Cumberland House. 2005. Book.

O'Kane, James M. Crooked Ladder: Gangsters, Ethnicity and the American Dream. Transaction Publishers. 2004. Book.

Blood, Roses & Valentines.
http://www.prairieghosts.com/valentine.html

Eig, Jonathan. The St. Valentine's Day Massacre – Excerpt from "Get Capone".
http://www.chicagomag.com/Chicago-Magazine/May-2010/Get-Capone-St-Valentines-Day-Massacre-Jonathan-Eig/

Waugh, Daniel. Egan's Rats: The Untold Story of the Gang that ruled Prohibition-era St. Louis. Cumberland House. 2007. Book.

Helmer, William and Bilek, Arthur J. The St. Valentine's Day Massacre: The Untold Story of the Bloodbath That Brought Down Al Capone. Cumberland House. 2004. Book.

Fred Killer Burke. The Outlaw Journals. 2006.
http://www.babyfacenelsonjournal.com/fred-burke.html

Fred "Killer" Burke.
http://www.myalcaponemuseum.com/id91.htm

Bourbon County.

http://genealogytrails.com/kan/bourbon/newsarticles1.html

www.ingramcontent.com/pod-product-compliance
Lightning Source LLC
Chambersburg PA
CBHW020303030426
42336CB00010B/881